SELF HELP

21 Self-Help Methods!

Self Help - Counseling To Overcome

Anxiety, Fear, Depression And Anger!

We have been there – and Escaped!

Now Helping others – is our Mission!

Table of Content

INTRODUCTION

I want to **congratulate** you for buying this book! Why? The best answer probably can be given with one of my favorite quotes (since the days my wife and I were fighting against her Anxiety & Depression):

"You cannot keep running away from your fears. At some point in Life you will have to build up the courage to face and overcome them. If possible – Forever!"

These few lines are so true and again: I congratulate you because buying this book you made the first Statement! "I do not accept my fears anymore! I do something to conquer them!"

"SELF HELP. 21 Self-Help Methods!".

This book contains our personal experience and research. We help you with an easy to follow step-by-step guide to show you exactly, how to overcome Anxiety, Fear, Depression and Anger. Using these steps will boost Your Happiness, Confidence and Motivation. With these powerful Life Hacks, Meditation Techniques and Quotes, your Life will start to change immediately **- and forever!**

Thanks again for buying this book; I hope you enjoy it and that it will have the best possible impact for your future!

Yours,
Dana & E.N. Richardson

FOREWORD

Why I wrote this book – together with my wife for you:

Do you know how it feels when Anxiety or Depression takes control? Oh yes**:** It Feels like I want to run away from myself; somehow escape from my body, my restless mind. - My thoughts torture me – circling like loud noise inside my head!

I know what you go through! My Wife was struggling with Anxiety & Depression but we fought, we learned and fought again. Finally - we managed to really FREE her. **And You can do it, too!**

We Want To Help You - To Help Yourself! PERIOD!

This is the simple goal – why we created the book Self Help for YOU! The self-help techniques we learned and discovered will help you on your journey – to **Conquer Your Fears and Get Rid of Anxiety, Depression and Anger!**

It was a pleasure creating this book and I hope that the self-help techniques discussed here helps you on your journey through a passionate and exciting life.

The techniques that you'll learn soon are not only good in chronic cases, but in one-off encounters as well. Everyone can benefit from the new thinking processes that you can develop by practicing these self-help methods. It will change your mind so that you can identify whether you're in a negative emotional state and help you heal yourself. If you do have chronic cases of anxiety, depression, fear, or anger, then you can use these techniques as often as you need to change your state of mind on demand.

My goal is to have you question your thinking so that you can identify and eliminate the negative ways of thinking that you adopt. After you have found ways to cope, then it's time to improve your thinking and build confidence in your abilities. You'll do this by changing your daily routine, practicing meditation, and being more mindful. Section II: Increasing The Positive will teach you 9 ways that you can lead a more happy, confident, and motivation rich life.

Keep an open mind when practicing these techniques. Continue the things that help you and ignore what doesn't bring you positive results. Nothing will work for everyone, since we are all individuals. But surely some of the tips listed in this simple self-help book will provide you with exactly what you need to experience new and exciting times in life. When you're ready to go on a new journey, go ahead and turn the page.

SECTION I:
LIMITING THE NEGATIVE

Anxiety, depression, anger, and fear are four of the most common negative emotions that people experience in their life. While many people can go about their day without being influenced strongly by their negative thoughts and feelings, the rest of us have to change or limit our actions because of negative emotion. Some people never find a way to get past their own minds, let alone allow another person to experience or help us with our imperfections.

Consider these facts:

- 350 million people of all ages experience depression throughout the world.

- 1 in 13 suffer from anxiety globally (including 10% of People in North America)

- ¾ of the US population has Glossophobia (fear of speaking in public).

- 68% of the US population has Necrophobia (fear of death).

- Slightly over ¼ of American's have Arachnophobia (fear of spiders).

Those are huge statistics that seem to explain that if you don't consider yourself to have anxiety, depression, or a combination of both; you probably have some fear that is irrational (and therefore have a type of anxiety). Fear is a good response when it's rational and based on stimuli presented at a certain time in your environment.

When anxiety however occurs in the mind when there is no stimuli present, triggering bodily responses that suggest you're actually in danger, that's when it's not positive. Anxiety occurs when someone says something, you feel a certain way, or something physically happens to you; but what you experience at that time isn't actually life threatening, which is the reason that anxiety is a brain disorder.

Now if you're sitting there thinking, "Well I don't want to speak in public, but I surely don't have Glossophobia," then your fear probably isn't irrational. If you could get up right now and give a short speech about how you're day went yesterday, but you just wouldn't enjoy it, then that's one thing. But most people will make life decisions and go out of their way to avoid their fear of an object or situation that's disproportional to the actual danger that could occur. That's what makes the fear a phobia, which is recognized as being irrational.

The truth of the matter is that most of the things you worry about statistically have less of a chance of occurring than a positive outcome. If you worry about things that have already occurred then you're not alone. This is a big source of fear but the truth is, the danger has already come and gone. Overall, 90% of the things that you fear aren't significant issues, and 88% of the things that you fear that is based on your health won't happen at all.

Keep this in mind for the upcoming chapters of this book. If you avoid certain places or activities because you believe that something negative will happen, consider whether that is rational. If you stress out about where your life is or is not at this current moment, instead of thinking about the negative, can you influence things for the better? More than likely if you believe that something positive will occur without focusing on the negative, that's what you'll bring into your life.

Now that you are armed with the correct mindset, let's get into the first four chapters of this section. Chapters 1 – 4 discuss anxiety, fear, depression, and anger respectively.

CHAPTER 1:
OVERCOMING ANXIETY

Everyone faces anxiety at a certain point in his or her life. It's a natural human emotion that could be triggered before attending a job interview, before taking an important test, or when you face a stressful problem at work. An anxiety disorder occurs in several different forms over at least a six-month period. Let's discuss the different types of anxiety disorders and some of the symptoms that you might face if you have anxiety.

General anxiety disorder, social anxiety disorder, panic disorder, and specific phobias are all types of anxiety disorders. These disorders interrupt your ability to live a happy and productive life and are considered a mental illness. The reasons that someone develops a mental illness like anxiety are unknown. Research has shown that mental illness is not due to a character flaw or personal weakness, but rather your environment and changes that occur in the brain, which influence how circuits communicate and send information.

Anyone can develop an anxiety disorder although it's slightly more common in women than men. Millions of people in the United States struggle with anxiety disorders, with most forming in early adolescence or adulthood. Anxiety disorders can bring one or a combination of the following symptoms depending on the type of disorder faced which include:

- Feelings of loss of control, fear, and panic

- Problems sleeping

- Compulsive behaviors

- Muscle Tension

- Heart palpitations

- Shortness of breath

- Nausea and dizziness

- Cold or clammy hands and feet

Modern day treatment of anxiety disorders mostly takes the form of medication and therapy. The goal of this section is to discuss methods of healing your body from the negative effects of anxiety through means of self-help. Here are three different methods that will help you if you face anxiety:

Lesson #1: Accept the fact that uncertainty exists.

Nothing happens at 100% certainty. Anxious people often try to figure out what's going to happen before a situation has even occurred as a method of preventing any negative outcome. Unfortunately, no one can accurately predict the future or control the outcome on an event. When you accept that uncertainty is a natural consequence of life, you're able to better cope with it.

Worrying about the outcome of something won't allow you to control the situation; it will actually cause you to avoid the situation or to go through increased anxiety if the outcome isn't the one you expect. Let's change how you see uncertainty.

First, begin by taking out a piece of paper. Answer the following questions as honestly as you can to change how you view uncertainty.

i.   Do you look at uncertainty as the cause of negative experiences?
ii. What is the chance that an uncertain event can have a neutral or positive outcome?
iii. Is it reasonable to think that bad events will occur because of uncertainty?
iv. Can you really be certain about every aspect of your life?

v.   Can you allow yourself to live with uncertainty since the likelihood of a negative event occurring is very small?

Taking a look at your views on these questions will hopefully allow you to take a look at your future actions. Instead of worrying about the things and outcomes you can't control, why not look for the little things that you can do instead? Are there some short-term things that you can do right now to make life a little easier or resolve any of your issues? Whenever you focus on something that is out of your control, your brain can't comprehend.

Whenever you notice that you are unable to live with uncertainty and have anxiety or worry because of this fact, think back to the answers you wrote. Unfortunately life isn't always great. When you focus on how to resolve any issues that come up in your life when they happen, instead of being anxious about avoiding potential negative outcomes, then you can control your world with more balance.

Lesson #2: Take a look at your thinking.

The reason that you are anxious, depressed, have low self-esteem, or face relationship conflict is often related to how you think. Your thinking is something that you need to control well when you have anxiety. The thoughts and beliefs that you hold which cause you to go into states of anxiety might actually be irrational cognitive distortions.

Cognitive distortions occur when you think irrationally about yourself and the things going on in the world around you. When your thinking is irrational, so is your behavior. When you learn to identify and adopt rational and objective thought processes, then you'll have positive emotional and behavioral experiences.

Whenever you become anxious about a thought that you hold, here are some questions you should ask yourself to identify if you are experiencing a cognitive distortion:

Is there actual evidence that my thoughts are true or untrue?

Can I look at the situation in a way that is positive or more realistic?

How likely is it that what I'm afraid of will actually occur?

What are the more likely outcomes?

How does this thought help me?

How does this thought hinder me?

Does worrying about this thought or outcome assist me?

What would I tell someone who was worrying about this thought?

These questions help you identify irrational thought. Hopefully it allows you to consider the things that you are worrying about so that you can move on and have positive experiences. In addition to questioning your thinking, you can also identify common cognitive distortions as they occur to you that increase anxiety. Here are some cognitive distortions that you might notice hindering you:

Labeling - One common cognitive distortion is to label things as being one thing or the other. If you make a mistake on an exam, you may say, "I'm stupid; I'm unable to learn; I'm a failure." The reality is that you are not defined by your experiences. You still have the ability to learn, grow, and succeed; and therefore should not label yourself negatively.

Emotional reasoning - The way you feel does not always reflect the actual reality of the situation. An example of this might be, "I'm fearful of my surroundings, therefore I'm in actual physical danger." You have to consider that sometimes how you feel and the reality of the situation don't match up.

Sometimes your emotions can be triggered by confusion, misunderstanding, and your own thoughts, and not on the actual reality of the situation.

Filtering your thoughts - Think back to all of the times where you have done anything. If you focus only on the few negative things, which occur in a situation, while ignoring all of the positive things, then you are filtering your thoughts. This is easy to do, however it's considered a cognitive distortion.

There are many more types of cognitive distortions that can affect you, especially if you face anxiety on a daily basis. Make sure that you learn about the other types of irrational thought processes so that you can identify the patterns of your own mind. When you're able to identify irrational thought then you can bring yourself back to a place of calm and happiness.

Lesson #3: Change your surroundings.

If the people who are in your life are the ones causing you to adopt a negative mental state, then you have to change the people who are around you. It's all too easy to adopt the emotions of another person. Some people are empathetic to strangers and can change mental states quickly when someone in their environment does too. Most people become upset, angry, or sad when someone close to us feels strong emotions as well.

You should really watch how other people influence your anxiety and be careful around those that have a big impact on your mental state. There are three ways that you can change your environment to help make your anxiety easier to control.

I. **Start keeping a journal.** Have you ever been here? Sometimes you're totally happy and content and then minutes later, it seems that your world is crashing down quickly. If you identify with this and have been triggered without understanding what the root cause of your new emotional imbalance is, then keeping a journal of your activities can help.

Discuss the before, during, and after of any episodes that you have. Read it when you have calmed down. When you're reading the events, try to identify any commonalities. It may help you uncover what is bringing on certain feelings and thoughts.

II. **Change the people around you.** If you notice through your journaling that you're anxious because of the people you're around then it's time to find a new support system.

That doesn't mean you have to give up old friends. You should however consider spending less time with people who bring about negative emotions, while increasing your time with family members and loved ones who understand what you face on a daily basis.

III. **Share your problems with a support system.** Not everyone can be included in your support system. You should have friends that you can share your feelings with while being supportive and gaining perspective. The wrong people to include in your support system are those that make you feel less worthy because of your fears and doubts – obviously this isn't the case.

Whether you have anxiety or not, these three tips can help you identify negative ways of thinking and develop you into a more loving individual. Outcomes in your life will never be certain. Does that mean you should stop taking risks? Of course not!

Once you're able to question your own thinking while identifying all of the potential outcomes instead of thinking only about the potential negative outcomes, then you're able to free your mind and make a decision. Remember that when you limit yourself to only seeing the negative in an object or situation then you also limit your own creativity.

Being free is seeing all of the potential possibilities and figuring out a way to reach the best possible outcome for you. This will help you try new things, meet new people, and truly change your environment. If you want to open your world to new sights and developments, then the first thing you should do is take a look at your beliefs, thoughts, and feelings, to learn how you can influence the world around you.

CHAPTER 2:
DEFEATING FEAR

Chances are that you have some sort of rational or irrational fear. The goal of this chapter is to help you overcome any of your fears so that you can make rational life decisions that help you accomplish your biggest goals. Some fear is a natural response in the brain, which changes the physical and mental state of the body. Any fear that occurs aside from bring in actual danger is unnatural and caused by a mental illness.

Rational fear is triggered as a direct result of being in a dangerous situation that can either bring pain or threat to your life. When there's something in your environment that can cause you pain or harm, then your body is built to increase blood flow, sweat, and raise your heart rate so that you can respond to the situation. Your body's natural response to fear is to prepare for battle or run away and hope that the danger doesn't kill you.

Irrational fear causes the same physical response, even when you're not presented with anything dangerous. A thought in your head, the words of another person, or a feeling that you have can trigger a fear response with your body. When you experience irrational fear it's consistent and doesn't pass easily. Then you begin intentionally avoiding places where you can encounter the object or situation, which only complicates your life.

Most of the time the object or situation that someone fears is actually unsafe in certain conditions. The difference with someone who dislikes spiders versus someone who has an irrational fear of spiders is that the person who dislikes spiders will go about their day regularly without thinking about encountering a spider. Their fear may only be triggered if they see one skimmer into a corner, but they'll continue to live their life after the spider is no longer visible.

On the other hand, if you have an irrational fear of spiders then you're going to avoid places that you think contains spiders. You're not going to look in your basement for months at a time. You might avoid taking walks in the summer months when spiders are spinning webs all around your neighborhood. You may even make sure that your home is fumigated every month so that you never witness the few spiders that inhabit your home.

These actions may seem extreme and in reality they are. After you've identified that you have a fear or phobia about something that is restricting what you do in life and stopping you from reaching your full potential, then it's time to change the way you think.

These three powerful lessons will help you overcome any fear, so that you can live a happy and successful life.

Lesson #4: Figure out the root cause of your fears.

Your fear is rooted in something that you believe is dangerous or that you believe will bring your pain or threat. Some fears are caused by the result of an action, instead of the action itself. For example, you might have been bitten by a spider as a young child and later developed a phobia toward spiders later in life. It isn't necessarily that you are afraid of the spider, you're just afraid of suffering the consequences of being bitten by a spider. Make sure that you identify and write down any past experiences you had with the things that you are afraid of as well as the root cause of your fear.

Lesson #5: Change your body and mind.

You are in control of your mind. Your mind can say, "I'm afraid of this object," just as easily as it can say, "I'm not afraid of this object". The difference all depends on the images and words that you create in your mind.

Begin by attempting to see things logically. If you are afraid of moths but dislike butterflies, why is this the case? Both flutter through the sky. It's just that there's a positive association with one and a negative connotation with the other. Think about the errors in your thinking when you encounter something that you're fearful of.

When you encounter that object or situation that brings you worry, try to breath deeply and relax. Allow your shoulders to relax and calm any areas of your body that are tense. Swish water around your mouth if you notice any dryness in your tongue. These simple techniques will combat the normal response that occurs in your body, while signaling to your brain that everything is under control.

Lesson #6: Use positive affirmations.

Tell yourself that you are not afraid of your fears. As simple as this sounds, it's actually very helpful when it comes to dealing with your fears. When you use positive affirmations you brain and body start to believe what you're saying and are less impacted by things that you are afraid of. Look at things in a positive light and point out some reasons why the things that you're afraid of are actually beneficial and helpful to your life.

Release the Power of Affirmations

Affirmations are positive statements we make and repeat to impress in our subconscious minds in order to affect a change. It is repeated in order to trigger the subconscious towards positive action. For affirmations to work they have to be repeated frequently. A practical example of affirmations and how they work is ... let's say you were in a race and you had to run 15 yards. Well by the 5thyard you start to feel tired but you keep saying to yourself "I can do this, I am going to finish" and you do! That is an example of how your mind propels you on to the end of the race.

What happens is that most of the time we repeat negative affirmations all the time. We say "I can't do that; that's impossible". As a result we have negativity and undesirable results in our lives. This is the power of the word. It can build or it can destroy. It's up to us how we use them. If we use them in a negative way or for negative intent that's just what it brings us. Many times we may repeat negative statements without even being conscious of it. If you tell yourself you can't do something over and over again you will fail. You are programming yourself to do so. The subconscious accepts anything we say negative or positive as truth. So if you understand this, then why not stay positive?

Affirmations function in the mind very much like programming a computer does. They work the same way creative visualization does. By repetition of a word or phrase you are focusing your aim, creating mental images that correspond in the conscious mind to the words or phrases. This in turn affects the unconscious mind. We "think" with our conscious minds first and then the subconscious takes over. By consciously using affirmations you are reprogramming your subconscious. This is the key to reshaping your external life and conditions for the better.

Sometimes we see results quickly, sometimes we don't. It depends on your goal. Some things, with quick re-programming, we can see immediately, some take time. Also keep in mind if you are positive only when you say the affirmations and then go back to negative mindsets then you are neutralizing your affirmations. You have to think positive to have positive results.

When you do affirmations it's important to say short phrases instead of long ones. In this way it is easier to remember. Repeat the phrases at any time; when you are on the bus, walking anywhere. Do not use them when you are driving or crossing the street. You have to use safety sense. It is suggested to repeat them for 5 to 10 minute sessions; several times a day. You must be in a physically and emotionally relaxed state; tension-free.

When you say the statements say them with conviction. Use only positive wording to describe what you want. For example if you want to lose weight don't say" I am Fat" say " I am getting slimmer" or " I am reaching my ideal weight". The second affirmations invoke positive images. Also affirm in the present tense not the future. For example if you say "I will be rich one day" that means you are not going to attain it in the immediate now. In cases like this, it is more effective to say "I am rich now". By stating what you want to be true in your life now the subconscious will work to make it happen in the conscious.

Here are some samples of positive affirmations:

- I am happy and healthy

- I am in control of my thought

- I trust my self

- I love being who I am

- I am a loveable person

- I love myself

- I am confident

- My Future will be bright because I work on it

- I am sailing on the river of happiness (can use river of anything you want)

- Talking to other people is easy for me

- I am motivated

- I love every new morning because it brings me the opportunity for a great day

- I get wealthier every day

- My body is healthy and functioning in a very good way

- I have a lot of energy

- I study and comprehend fast

- My mind is calm

- I am calm and relaxed in every situation

- My thoughts are under my control

- I radiate love and happiness

- I am surrounded by love

- I have the perfect job for me

- I am living in the house of my dreams

- I have good and loving relationships with my husband/wife

- I have a wonderful and satisfying job

- I have the means to travel abroad whenever I want to

- I am successful in whatever I do

- Everything is getting better every day

Take these just as examples. The real power of affirmations will be released, if you utilize those affirmations – you really trust in from the bottom of your heart! Write them on cards and take these cards with you.

Everytime you feel negative thoughts or emotions overwhelm – read your cards and force yourself to smile. My wife needed about 3 weeks. After these even thinking of these cards made her mood shift immediately. Repetition, repetition, repetition. You can do this!

When you use these techniques, your fears might not be dispelled right away. Continue to practices these lessons enough overtime and notice how it changes your thought process as well as your actions.

CHAPTER 3:
COPING WITH DEPRESSION

Depression is a severe psychiatric problem that is often developed from anxiety and fear. It causes feelings of hopelessness and despair that often interferes with the ability to do everyday tasks. Some people face a single interaction with depression at a certain point in life, while others experience depression as an ongoing lifetime issue. The goal of this section is to help you identify depression and learn how to cope with the symptoms that it brings.

Some symptoms that may suggest that you have depression include social withdrawal, intense mood swings, poor sleep, fatigue, and thoughts of suicide. Psychotic depression is also a major issue that can cause hallucinations and delusions. These symptoms are usually caused by the depression, reflecting and magnifying feelings of despair and negative emotions instead of being caused by a significant brain disorder.

When you suffer from depression over long periods of time, then it's possible you have dysthymia. Dysthymia is a form of chronic depression that causes feelings of unhappiness, but usually doesn't affect a person's ability to function normally. There's also seasonal affective disorder, which affects an individual at the same time each year, normally when the seasons change. Major depressive disorder is your standard level of depression that doesn't normally occur at a set point in life, but causes either a single incident of depression or a series of depressive bouts.

Depression is very complicated and there usually isn't just one event that causes someone to develop depression. It's a cause of biological, environmental, and emotional factors that may occur after a significant event just as likely as it occurs seemingly at random. Just because there is no "apparent" reason to develop depression doesn't mean that you can't develop it at some point in your life.

Your standard treatment for depression includes taking antidepressant medications. Some people also take other drugs such as antipsychotic medications to fight their depression. Luckily, if you are averse to seeking out medication for your natural body response to environmental, biological, and emotional stimulus, then there are other alternatives for you.

You can do things such as change your diet, exercise more, meditate, create meaningful relationships, and challenge your own thoughts. Here are three helpful lessons that you should include to your life whenever you feel an onset of depression so that you can change your mind and enjoy life.

Lesson #7: Experience your environment.

It's not easy to feel up to doing anything when you're depressed. As much as you want to just stay in bed or lock yourself in your room, this often doesn't work because you'll likely stay in your head during this time. Sometimes a change of environment is all that you need to experience in order to feel better emotionally.

Exercise is one way that you can start coping with your depression. It doesn't have to involve going to a gym everyday if that's not your thing. You can simply go for a walk to the park, go for a bike ride, or jog around your neighborhood. Studies have shown that exercise is just as powerful as medication when it comes to dealing with depression. It will also help you sleep easier through the night and increase your energy levels altogether.

The recommended amount of daily exercise for most people is 30 minutes a day. That doesn't mean you have to jump right into doing rigorous exercise right away. Start small and build your way up. Attend classes where you move your body, if you enjoy doing yoga or even martial arts. Go swimming, play tennis, or just participate in an activity that makes you feel happy. That's the key to sticking with exercise in the long run.

You also don't have to exercise for thirty minutes straight. When you're feeling low, go for a walk for 5 to 10 minutes. This should help you feel better for at least a couple hours. If your negative emotions or thoughts come back, all you have to do is go for another walk and notice how much better you feel. Put on your favorite music, exercise with a friend, or enjoy the company of your favorite animal, and what might be difficult to do at first will become a fun activity for all.

Lesson #8: Question your thinking.

Everything that you go through while you're depressed might naturally seem negative. You might ask, "why me," or "why am I always put in these horrible situations?" Although these might occur naturally, you should consider your life and the situations that you find yourself in to discover if you can be optimistic or neutral about the things that happen around you.

For every negative thought that pops into your head, try and come up with a reason to see the situation in a positive light. Start by thinking outside of yourself. If the events that caused you to think negatively happened to someone else, would you still hold the same point of view? It's possible that you would, but it's also possible that you can find a silver lining in the events that take place when you look at it from an outsider's perspective.

If you're the cause of your negative emotion then maybe you're holding yourself to a standard that's too high. Many depressed people consider themselves perfectionists and don't like to disappoint themselves or others. When your life isn't exactly where you want it to be, instead of going deeper into depression, be less hard on yourself and consider all of the wonderful attributes that you have.

Don't forget to socialize with the right people. Ask them how they would feel in your situation. Consider what they say and ask for feedback as to what they would do in that situation as well. Perhaps they can give you the perspective that you need in order to get over your depressed emotions. Try to be as optimistic as possible when you're speaking to people that are your emotional support, pick the people who you discuss your problems with well, and take their suggestions to heart. They might just offer an overlooked solution that helps you get out of your rut.

Lesson #9: Do the things that you love to do.

When you ignore your true feelings and lose track of what makes you happy, then it's easy to fall into depression. Start filling your time with people and activities that bring you enjoyment. Also make sure that you take care of your body well by watching what you eat, getting the adequate amount of sleep, and enjoying the sunlight a little bit each day.

One thing that helps a lot of people with depression is having a pet. You can't replace human connection with anything else, but having companionship can help you feel more connected to others. It also allows you to spend more time outside and boosts the amount of joy that you have for life.

Hopefully these simple tips will help you cope with depression. They're easy to include to your daily routine for a reason and you can use these techniques whenever you're motivated to. Simply getting in touch with your passions by watching a funny movie, reading a good book, or taking a nice relaxing bath is often enough to change your mood for the better so that you can get back to your normal life.

CHAPTER 4:
OUTDOING ANGER

Anger is another emotion that people naturally feel in reaction to the environment and situations around them. It causes physiological and biological changes in the body by triggering a fight or flight response, much like anxiety, but instead of causing fear or worry, it results in irritation, rage, and fury. Internal and external events can cause anger, which is usually based on previous events or traumatic memories, so it's important to identify the cause of any anger you experience.

The main way that an individual reacts to anger is through aggression. This is natural because your situation might call for a sudden response in order to protect yourself or your loved ones. The healthy way to deal with anger is through being assertive instead of aggressive, so that you can fix the situation you find yourself in without harming yourself or others. Being assertive allows you to solve your issues while being respectful and doesn't call for attacking or demanding something from another individual.

This chapter will introduce new techniques to deal with anger so that if you notice yourself being aggressive, you can change your thoughts and actions to a form that's more productive. That doesn't mean that you should try to hold on to or suppress your anger, but rather that you should find a new way to deal with your problems that's constructive.

When you hold in your anger, you're more likely to get upset with yourself, which brings about a number of biological and physiological issues to your body. It can also cause you to act in a non-constructive way that's passive-aggressive, cynical, or hostile. People who don't learn to control their anger in a positive way end up destroying their relationships and themselves. That's why it's important to calm down, look at your internal responses, deal with the issue appropriately, and let the feelings subside.

Managing your anger can be difficult, but it isn't impossible. Participating in anger management allows you to reduce the physical and emotional response that your body goes through in a timely manner when it counts. It's important to understand that you can't always change the people who are around you or avoid the things that make you upset, but you can control your own actions when something comes up.

Unlike with many mental illnesses, you don't need other people to tell you when you have an anger issue. You probably have already realized it yourself. That's the first step to controlling it in a positive way. All people have different temperaments and become angry at different things and show their anger differently. Some people are naturally hotheaded when a negative event occurs, while others might show their anger by being grumpy or irritable. If you withdrawal socially or become physically ill when you're upset, this can be just as detrimental as lashing out at others or making your anger apparent. These three lessons will help you cope with your anger.

Lesson #10: Try to relax.

This is especially important if you're in a relationship with another person who also has a hot temper. Cultivating relaxation in stressful situations takes time to develop, but with enough practice, you'll be able to do it. Find something that helps you relax and return to it whenever you notice yourself becoming upset. Some simple things that you can try include:

Breathing deeply and letting your body relax before deciding on an appropriate response.

Thinking in a calm manner by reminding yourself to relax, or even counting to ten is the best basic concept to feel better. You can repeat this process as much as needed in the moment to calm down.

Make calm movements. Learning yoga or meditation can help you calm your mood and make good choices whenever you find yourself upset.

Lesson #11: Learn to communicate.

Disputes normally erupt when one party doesn't understand or misunderstands what another person is suggesting. Make sure that you get a full picture of something before you jump to a conclusion and act. Slow down, think about what the other people that have created the conflict are saying, and discover a way to resolve the issue without becoming enraged. Take your time before responding to someone who has upset you and act in a calm manner.

Share your frustrations with another person if you need to. Sometime people do or say things that make you unhappy without realizing it. There's only one way to correct a dispute that you have with another person and that involves talking through it. Don't retaliate if the other person doesn't understand you or gets defensive. Chances are that the other person just wants to be understood or share a deeper connection to understand what you're going though.

Lesson #12: Reconstruct your mind.

Basically, you should think though you anger and ask yourself if it's appropriate to feel the way that you do about your situation. Avoid doing anything that will just make another person more enraged such as using swear words or threatening action. Learn how to let small things go. You don't always have to get your way and you'll be a much bigger person by learning how to walk away from confrontation if it isn't worth it.

Make sure that your thoughts are rational and that you aren't acting irrationally. When you increase your anger, then you're more likely to do something that only makes matters worse. Anger itself won't solve any problems; it will actually make you feel worse. There are better ways to come to an agreement than by using anger, and by solving the issue first in your mind, you'll be able to influence the minds of others.

Whenever you need to come back to these lessons, do so. Life is an ongoing experience, so you'll likely experience your anger again. If you learn how to work constructively, then your anger won't lead to any irrational actions and you won't have to suffer the consequences either. In fact, you can probably resolve the problem quickly and safely by learning how to control your mind.

SECTION II:
INCREASING THE POSITIVE

Now that you've learned how to deal with any emotional issues that you face on a daily basis, it's time to learn how to increase the positive in your life. When you aren't inhibited by anger, anxiety, depression, or fear then you're able to live the life of your dreams. It will take self-control and dedication, but with enough hard work you can accomplish everything that you want in life.

You'll begin by learning how to allow happiness in your life. Everyone wants nothing but happiness and success, but sometimes our own mind stops us from achieving that. Since you have dispelled fear and worry, you should have all the necessary tools to step out of your comfort zone and accomplish things that you never considered possible. That's the subject of **Chapter 5 – Allowing Happiness in Your Life.**

Once you learn three techniques to cultivating happiness, you can build up your confidence. You grow your confidence by doing what you love and making progress toward your goals and dreams one step at a time. It doesn't matter how slowly you make progress. As long as you are doing something that you are passionate about, you'll end up being great at that. Confidence builds over time as you begin to understand your strengths and weaknesses. With every minor success that you have, you'll build a great foundation that allows you to grow and develop even more. That's what you'll learn to do in **Chapter 6 – Creating Confidence.**

Chapter 7 – Being Moved By Motivation will show you simple ways to motivate yourself to lead an amazing life. These lessons will stop you from burning out and give you the fuel to continue on with any endeavor. Following your passion can be difficult at times when you feel the pressure to earn an income, spend time with other people, or deal with your other daily responsibilities. When you're ready how to juggle it all and not go crazy in the process, flip to the next page.

CHAPTER 5:
ALLOWING HAPPINESS IN
YOUR LIFE

Wherever you look, there seems to be new information that is filled with negativity. Sure, you won't be able to live a happy life for every moment of your existence, but that doesn't mean you shouldn't strive to be happy with everything that you do. Happiness is within your grasp and it's very important to leading a life that you want.

Even though it's easy to forget to be happy, your own happiness is incredibly important. When you're happy it influences everything about you. You have a longer life expectancy, you feel healthier, and you spread that joy and wonder on to other people who are involved in your life. Being happy will allow you to find new ways of being creative, retain your youth, and even financially successful.

Imagine a world where everyone was happy. Think about all the amazing achievements people could accomplish, the changes that would occur in everyone's life, and the irrational violence and oppression that would end. Happiness doesn't only affect you; it also benefits every single being on the earth.

Before you can accomplish the goals that you've set, first you have to be happy. The same goes for feeling accomplished and successful. The key is to do what you love while spreading happiness to others. All that's needed to change the minds of others is a little bit of happiness, and everything else will align automatically. Once you realize this, you have gained a lot of constructive power that can be a force for good.

If you want to find happiness, you first must understand that it can be obtained. It's totally in your reach and it's actually the natural state of being. The reason that you aren't happy all of the time is because of negative thought. The outside world does a great job of influencing our thoughts and situations that we find ourselves in. When you release the hold that negative thinking has on you, then you're able to return to your natural state of bliss.

Of course, it takes time to get used to happiness. Feelings of anger, worry, depression, and fear get in the way. Sometimes you may even feel as if it isn't right to be doing so well. That's when self-sabotage kicks in and you fall into old negative habits that hinder your progress. The good news is that when you identify yourself returning to things that are no longer serving you, then you also have the power to change yourself for the better.

Understand that no one but you can determine your happiness. No one has the power to make you feel anything but yourself. Anger and other negative emotions and thoughts might be triggered by the outside world but that's only if you lose control of your mind and allow it to happen. When you change the way that you are influenced by your surroundings then you'll have the power to always be happy. Let's discuss some methods you can use to find happiness.

Lesson #13: Find your purpose.

Finding your purpose takes time to discover. For some, it comes naturally and they embody their passion from day one. For the rest of us, we have to experience new things, participate in activities we don't enjoy and discover the things that we love to do. To begin figuring out what your purpose is, come up with a reason for your purpose in the first place.

Some of us want to help countless people who exist now and in the future. Others want to lead a happy life so they can oversee the success of their family. Take out the journal that you created in the first chapter (or start one right now,) and write down why you want to find your life purpose. The goal is for you to jump out of bed in the morning because you're so excited to live your passion. Take all the time you need to determine what your passion is and don't be afraid to experience many things before settling on the right idea.

Lesson #14: Push yourself to new heights.

If you want to live your passion, then you have to be willing to make sacrifice.

That includes:

- Taking the time to locate your one true life passion.

- Working tirelessly to accomplish great feats in your passion.

- Believing in the fact that you can live your life purpose to the fullest.

- Making the necessary positive changes to your life in order to create your best life.

- Allowing yourself to shape your own destiny by finding your life purpose.

Keep these as simple rules for your life and you'll have the power to change your life. Be happy with what you've accomplished, because it's further than most people go in their lives. Now that you know the basic things that you'll have to do and give up, it's time to push yourself to new heights.

When you begin any task, it's going to be difficult at first. Remember to be patient with yourself as what you're doing might bring fear or doubt. That's the natural feeling of the unknown, which passes every time that you do something that you're unfamiliar with. Calm yourself internally whenever you have negative beliefs. Continue on with your work no matter what comes up internally or externally, and have the dedication to continue on with your passion.

Lesson #15: Accept change.

The biggest determinant of whether you'll fail or succeed is the amount of action that you put toward your passions. If you put things off instead of getting up and doing the things that you need to, you won't progress as much as you have to in order to live a passionate life. The last thing you want to do for your happiness is shut yourself down before even starting.

Start by looking at your passion as an ongoing goal. You'll have to learn new skills and develop yourself in order to be the best person that you can. You'll also have to move outside of your comfort zone until you can afford to have another person complete the things that you don't want to. Get comfortable with being uncomfortable at first, since you'll learn even more about yourself, and might even end up finding something that you're even more passionate about then you first believed.

As you continue on your journey toward happiness by developing your skills and living a life of passion, you'll automatically begin to zone in on the things that you enjoy in life. You'll connect with new people, share new experiences, and develop your talents to a level that you're proud of. No matter what gets in your way, when you include happiness in your everyday routine, you'll find the passion and the strength to move on.

CHAPTER 6:
CREATING CONFIDENCE

As you realize more of your goals and dreams through time, your confidence will slowly build. Give yourself the time that you need to strengthen your confidence, especially if you're starting at a place with negative or neutral beliefs about what is possible for you. No matter what your background is, what life circumstances have influenced you thus far, or what people say to you; you can be a success. Let's discuss the different ways that you can build confidence and become the person that you were always meant to be.

Lesson #16: Set life goals.

Setting goals is the way to achieve anything you want in life. Make sure that you set all the goals that you have in your journal. It doesn't matter if it's the smallest goal you've ever set, or one that will take decades to accomplish. The more small goals you accomplish, the more you'll also progress your larger goals. As you accomplish more and more goals, your confidence will grow with you.

Break your large goal into smaller goals that are easier to achieve. That way, even your largest goal will only be a collection of small things that you can do. The smaller the goal, the easier it is to achieve, and the more you can accomplish all of the other tasks that you have to do each day.

Always plan out the day that you want to have tomorrow. You can plan out your day before you go to bed, or before the end of the workday – whichever works best for you. When you know exactly what it is that you want to do, then that gives your day meaning and the world becomes a lot less distracting. Overtime your confidence will find new heights and you'll realize that even the largest dreams are within your reach.

Lesson #17: Always expect success.

Success is a choice. You can resolve to succeed, or you can decide that you fail. Only you make that distinction in your life, and only you can give up on yourself. It doesn't matter how many jobs you've been fired from, how many companies you burnt into the ground, or how many times you've been told that you're not worthy to be where you are. If you choose success, no matter how many hardships appear in your life, you'll find a way to be successful. It's that simple.

Lesson #18: Practice confidence.

Ever heard the term "fake it 'til you make it?" That's absolutely true. When someone meets you for the first time, they know nothing about you. They don't know how much debt your in, whether you graduated from college, or what problems you face on the day-to-day. If you act like a confident individual who is happy to experience life with another person, then that's what they'll see.

Practice being confident in everything you do. That also includes knowing when to ask for help. You aren't alone in the world and you aren't expected to do everything on your own. Asking for help, learning new things for yourself, and greeting new people respectfully shows that you are confident in all aspects of your life, no matter what personal hardship you are facing.

Positivity When Abused

I am often asked how my wife did it to stay positive, even when she may gone through an abusive situation or have once been the victim of abuse. How does positivity fit in a person's life who has been damaged by hurt upon hurt for no apparent reason other than being alive? It is a fact that the emotional scars of abuse do last for years. The best thing an abused person can do is to try the best way to heal themselves through shedding all the negative programming shoved into them to accept the abuse. This way they can begin to heal. Many times years of abuse strips a human being of their sense of self and of their esteem.

The abused may even take responsibility and say it's their fault for the abuse which is what the abuser wants and is ridiculous to say the least. It is this very thinking that allows the victim to stay caught in the abuser's web. It allows the negative thoughts to take hold and stay with the victim sometimes their whole lives if it's not addressed. The first thing a victim of abuse has to do in order to heal and move on into a positive direction is to learn to face their past; accept the reality that it happened and then point themselves in a positive direction from that point in their lives. The victim must understand that no abuse is their fault and no one deserves to be abused period.

One way to start to turn away, in a positive fashion-form of abuse, is to look at the abusive situation differently. Would you allow someone you love or your best friend to take responsibility for being abused or allow the abuse to be done to them at all if you knew about it? Of course you wouldn't. You would make it known to them that they are a person of worth and do not deserve abuse under any circumstances.

Being a victim of abuse who reaches towards positivity is like someone climbing out of darkness. Have you ever felt your eyes blur and tear when you stay in a dark room too long and then go outside into a sunny day? You have trouble seeing at first and may cover your eyes from the sun rays. Then, while standing there, you gradually remove your hands that shade the eye and your eyes open fully and you are standing with your eyes wide opened in the sun. Well, this is the same way an abused person reacts to healing and positivity. They may reject it first or not know how to respond first but then get the idea and embrace it.

If you are a victim of abuse, you may not be able to control the thoughts and actions of those around you but you can control your own responses to them. The first thing you have to do is to declare that you are a survivor and then lift yourself up to a higher level. No one can keep you down unless you allow them to. It is easier said than done, especially if you fear for your life or the life of a loved one but it can be done. Abusers count on fear and immobilized beings to kick. If you have been able to break free of abuse even by running away (because you fear for your safety) or getting help from authorities you are one step closer to regaining yourself back.

You may also be long rid of your abusers, but it still takes time to heal emotional scars. Everyone heals at a different speed--there is no right or wrong way. A person that was abused must first and far most remind themselves that others have made it through and so will they. Also keep in mind many abused people who recover become better people for the experience believe it or not. You must remind yourself to focus on the positives in yourself(even the fact you survived the abuse) and leave the negative thought patterns behind as you do.

Just as with programming positivity in the mind for all of us the abused person must also do so. In doing so, they must let go of the painful past and its conditioning as well to free them to start over. As the victim does so, they are regaining control over their lives. The next important thing is for them to have faith in themselves and their strengths. It takes a strong person to over-come abuse on any level. As you focus on rising above the abuse you endured, you start to meet the positive goals you set for yourself.

Here are some things a victim can do to let positivity into their lives:

- Avoid negative people and situations like the plague; if it doesn't feel right stay clear.

- Stop dwelling in the past (easier said than done) by looking forward to a better future. Do this by setting new positive goals for yourself.

- When the negative thoughts creep in replace them with positive ones and remind yourself of them when you have to.

- Surround yourself with positive people.

- Try and find humor in things.

- Join a group or an activity that is positive.

- Do Not Allow Yourself to Be Labeled.

- Learn to accept compliments.

- Talk to a counselor, get into a support group.

- Read and do things on building self esteem.

To rid your life of abuse it's about over-coming those negative patterns that enabled the abuse in the first place. Over-coming abuse is a complex process. It can be very difficult and painful for the victim to handle the healing involved. Many times this is due to the overtly negative, critical and psychologically damaging thoughts that the abuser plants in their victims minds to control them. There is no quick fix to heal a victim of abuse; it's a process and takes work to bring positivity and light back to someone who has been in darkness and pain for sometimes years on end or their whole lives.

Self-esteem is the main thing to rebuild in order to reinstate positivity in a person of abuse's life. It is self esteem that virtually affects every aspect of our lives. How we feel and see ourselves affects our choices, our abilities to give and receive love and gives us the fortitude to change things when they need to be changed. So in order for positivity to set into a person who was a victim of any abuse they must incorporate positive mental exercises into the healing process. Abusers thrive on criticism and destroying the victims self esteem. So the abused has to fight to regain this back.

Because of the constant degradation involved in abuse, the victim becomes critical of themselves as well; so, some of the negative patterns that have to be changed, have to do with self-criticisms.

Ways to combat self-criticism is through:

- First notice how often you are self critical. When you are self critical you are basically doing the same thing the abuser did to you. You are in essence re-abusing yourself and lowering your own worth and esteem.

- Catch yourself when you are in a self critical or negative thought about yourself. Ask yourself "Whose voice am I hearing when I say this about myself?

- Focus on your positive aspects instead of dwelling on your faults. No one is perfect. Self-criticism can be damaging enough, but if you never give yourself credit for what you do have that's positive then you are in a devastating mode.

So, if you can do the first three things; you can now also include some self esteem building in the mix.

Here are some things to focus on:

- Set realistic and reachable goals. Both abusers and victims set unrealistic impossible high standards for themselves which is why the victim fails. In order to feel successful which is vital to one's self esteem set doable small goals that you can succeed in.

- Stop comparing yourself to others. This sets you up to feel less than adequate and the person you are comparing yourself to as better.

- Begin to nurture yourself. Disappointment comes when those who we think are supposed to nurture us don't. So do it yourself for yourself. No one can make up for the sense of deprivation someone feels or experienced and you can't expect someone to do it for you.

These are some simple things you can do to help change a negative mindset into a positive one. Like I said, it is not easy and it takes time. Go easy on yourself and incorporate these little things until they become automatic. You will notice that you are taking your life back when you do these things without having to make an effort. You are bringing positivity to yourself which is your deserved right.

CHAPTER 7:
BEING MOVED BY MOTIVATION

If you've made it this far, chances are that you've come all this way because you found the motivation to accomplish your goals and dreams. This section is really a bonus that I've included to help you stay motivated during tough times. Everyone experiences different things throughout life; some good, some bad. How you choose to look at it is up to you. What you do with your life after experiencing negative and positive things defines who you are as a human being.

Let's discuss a few lessons on how to stay motivated, so that you can live your ultimate life.

Lesson #19: Have a goal that's larger than you.

If you want to achieve your passion, then you have to have a reason that exceeds your life. Perhaps you want to live your passions so that your children have a good role model. Maybe you want to become a vegan activist so that you save the environment and make the world a place where all creatures thrive. The point is that you shouldn't just work for the benefit of yourself, but the benefit of those you care about and all of humanity.

Lesson #20: Reflect on where you've gone.

When you've built up your confidence, probably you wouldn't take no for an answer. Life is made up of defining moments. There will be times where you are pushed to move away from your dreams. If you slip, then you may just fall into old habits. That's why it's important to reflect on what you've accomplished and decide not to ever move back to previous ways of thinking. The more that you reflect on why you're doing what you're doing, the easier it will be for you to continue on that route.

CONCLUSION

Lesson #21: Celebrate where you are.

Congratulations on making it this far toward accomplishing your dreams. Even if this is only your first time reading this book, make sure that you pat yourself on the back (at least, I recommend going on a date with yourself.). Most people don't look for the solutions to their life problems. Most people also don't try and find success that they know lies inside.

Fortunately, you aren't like most people. You are on a journey that allows you to break free from your mind and the influence of others. Now go out and accomplish what you were put on this earth to do!

If you need a simple way of looking at your fears, try this approach, which really helped my wife a lot:

"**F-E-A-R** has two meanings:

1. Forget Everything **A**nd **R**un   or
2. Face Everything **A**nd **R**ise."   _Zig Ziglar

**Rise from now on –
You already made a great Start!**

A FEW WORDS FROM THE AUTHOR: E.N. RICHARDSON

Dear Reader of this book.

Thank You! For your support and trust – buying this book! I really hope that I was able to help you. Stay on your path of Self-Improvement and Fighting your Fears. There is no other secret to becoming happy again than this. Use these techniques on a regular basis and you will succeed! My wife and I experienced ourselves what a great impact this can have on your future. I once read a quote from someone that I carry with me and that I want to share with you:

'If you are willing to do the work – You can have everything you want!'_ unknown author

You bought this book – this shows that you are willing to do the work. You are ahead of so many other people because, most people only want to improve and succeed, but are not willing to do whatever it takes to achieve it! Keep working on yourself!

If you need more valuable tips to improve yourself take a look at my other books down below! Or visit my authors page on Amazon. Just type in Author and E. N. Richardson

All the best for you!

I highly appreciate your support by leaving a **Review on Amazon**.

This really helps!"

Yours

E. N. Richardson

A FEW WORDS FROM THE PUBLISHER:

be-to-ce publishing

We are very proud working together with bestselling author E.N. Richardson and want to thank him for – publishing his fourth book with us! Please support the author by giving an honest Review: *On Amazon*

We want to thank you for your trust, becoming one of our customers. We send out our Newsletter on a regular basis with Free Books from our portfolio for you. Just subscribe and watch out for the next books to com. From children´s books, romance, Science-fiction to business and self-development – books you will find anything!

Just visit http://be-to-ce.com
then Click Printing and Publishing

If you have any further questions around this book or the author, feel free to connect with us at anytime. For contact details: http://be-to-ce.com

EMOTIONAL INTELLIGENCE (EQ)
7 effective Methods & EQ Secrets!
Leverage Your Success & Happiness!

Simple Life Changer!

1. Release Your Power of Emotional Intelligence
2. Understand Yourself and Others Better
3. Improve Your Success in Managing Your Relationships
4. proven for Business and Private
5. 7 effective methods to Master your Emotional Intelligence

Limited Time Offer: - Check on Amazon –

Powerful Mindset Tricks To Immediately Create a Happy and Successful Future!

What you Think, you Become!

Learn in 21 practical Lessons how to boost Your Happiness & Success!
Section I: Change Your Mindset Toward Yourself
Section II: Change Your Mindset Toward Others
Section III: Become a better You!
Section IV: Change Your Money Mindset

Limited Time Offer: <u>- Check on Amazon –</u>

Reference Guide to Communication
How to Win Friends and
Master to Lead Conversations.

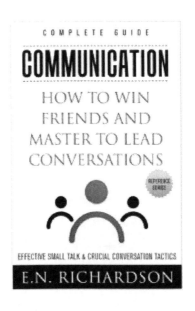

1. Rock-solid advice that carried thousands of people up the ladder of success
2. in their business and personal lives
3. How to make people like you instantly
4. How to win people to think your way
5. How to never run out of words again
6. How to change peoples behavior – the smart way

Limited Time Offer: Check on Amazon

"You cannot find Peace

by avoiding Life!"

-

"But you can find Peace,

Success and Happiness

Working on - Yourself!"

- E.N. Richardson -

Print: Start helping Yourself – I believe deeply that you can. – Trust Yourself!

NOTES from the book:

What do I want to achieve?

What are my daily tasks to get full control over my Life?

What are my new Goals to Achieve?

Which Lesson will have the greatest impact on these goals??

within is the solitary and utter responsibility of the recipient reader. Under no circumstances will any legal responsibility or blame be held against the publisher for any reparation, damages, or monetary loss due to the information herein, either directly or indirectly.

Respective authors own all copyrights not held by the publisher.

The information herein is offered for informational purposes solely, and is universal as so. The presentation of the information is without contract or any type of guarantee assurance.

The trademarks that are used are without any consent, and the publication of the trademark is without permission or backing by the trademark owner. All trademarks and brands within this book are for clarifying purposes only and are the owned by the owners themselves, not affiliated with this document.

71350738R00042

Made in the USA
Middletown, DE
23 April 2018